Looking Back Moving Forward

A MEMOIR OF HEALING AND TRANSFORMATION

KAREN A MACE

Companion Workbook

LOOKING BACK MOVING FORWARD

DEVOTIONAL WORKBOOK

Second Edition 2021

 KAREN MACE

www.karenmace.com
Copyright 2022 Karen Mace

All rights reserved.

No part of this publication may be reproduced, stored in, or introduced into a retrieval system, or transmitted in any form, or by any means (electronic, mechanical, photocopying, recording or otherwise) without the prior written permission of the author.

Unless otherwise indicated, all Scripture quotations are from the Amplified Bible. Copyright 1954, 1958, 1962, 1964, 1965, 1987 by The Lockman Foundation. Used by permission (www.Lockman.org). All rights reserved.

Scripture quotations marked NCV are taken from the New Century Version®. Copyright © 2005 by Thomas Nelson. Used by permission. All rights reserved.

Crafted Prayer by Graham Cooke used with permission of Brilliant Bookhouse. All rights reserved.

Cover design: Nikola Boskovski
Layout: Nikola Boskovski
Cover photo copyrights: Maria Nurince Domingas-Shutterstock.com
Published by: Karen Mace
ISBN Paperback: 978-0-6455194-0-2

 @KARENMACEWRITER  @KARENMACEWRITER  KARENMACE.COM

CONTENTS

Foreword	4
Before You Begin	5
Conquering Fear	7
Understanding Love	14
Freedom	23
Trust	31
Transformation – The Inging Principle	36
Resources	47
Afterword	56

FOREWORD

WELCOME TO THE
LOOKING BACK MOVING FORWARD
DEVOTIONAL WORKBOOK.

After the first version of Looking Back Moving Forward was published, a number of people who read the book told me they used it as a study, some individually and others in a group context. Then I had requests for a study book that would help readers delve more deeply into themes that run through the book. The thought became persistent, although not so much for a study book as for a devotional journal. And that's how this workbook came about.

This Workbook then, is for you if you want to explore, in more depth, the themes that are present in Looking Back Moving Forward. It will work equally well for you if you want to work alone with God on what He has shown you as you have read the book, as it will if you want to go deeper into those themes with a small group.

I trust you will find this helpful in your personal transformation journey with God.

Karen

Karen Mace

BEFORE YOU BEGIN

If you have picked up this workbook to accompany your reading of Looking Back Moving Forward, or once you've finished the book, I believe it is because God prompts you to do so. I trust that, as you respond to His prompting, God will do great things in your life through it.

To get the most from the workbook you should read Looking Back Moving Forward. There are five chapters in the workbook, and four of these correspond to chapters in the book, while the final chapter is a broader perspective of what a life of transformation means.

Throughout the workbook you will find:

- Truths to Treasure - related promises and principles from God's Word. I encourage you to meditate on the message of each of these Scriptures. Memorise them if you can. Meditation has the power to change your brain. As you meditate on God's Word, the Truth of it sets you free in many ways. We're seeing the evidence of this in scientific studies.

- Dig Deeper - creative activities designed to help give you an even richer understanding of what it means to be free in Christ. In my journey to freedom, God led me to study what is called Expressive Writing. We know now, and science is demonstrating this, that expressive writing can powerfully influence our overall wellbeing. It can benefit us mentally, physically, emotionally and spiritually. If you consider yourself more an artist, in that you prefer to draw rather than write, feel free to interpret the question and your response through whatever artistic form that best helps you make sense of it all.

- Information about how our brain is changed by our view of God.

- Express Your Experience - at the end of each chapter there is space for you to journal your thoughts, feelings and anything Holy Spirit reveals to you. I encourage you to take the time to write in this section as these entries can be amazingly revealing; priceless in fact!

> "May God grant you a spirit of wisdom and revelation [of insight into mysteries and secrets] in [deep and intimate] knowledge of Him, by having the eyes of your heart flooded with light, so that you can know and understand the hope to which He has called you, and how rich is His glorious inheritance in the saints…"
>
> I Ephesians 1: 17-18 AMP

I SUGGEST YOU...

- Read the corresponding chapter, where there is one, in Looking Back Moving Forward.

- Begin and end each of your sessions with prayer. Invite Holy Spirit to bring His discernment and wisdom to bear on what you are doing, to be very much a part of your devotional time. He will teach you and guide you into truth (see John 16:13). If you ask Him, He will give you insight and understanding, and He will also help you to hold those truths in your heart permanently - make sure you ask!

- Beginning with prayer also has the effect of bringing you into a place where you are receptive to learning new things, to revelation that might come. We know from research that prayer has the potential to positively affect parts of the brain associated with anxiety, depression, social awareness and empathy among other things. It has a calming effect. However, and this is important, YOU MUST COME WITH THE INTENTION to discover something new.

- Pace yourself - don't try to do too much at once. It is hard work if you are working on growth and transformation through healing. Expect to feel tired and to have some emotional ups and downs, and also to notice some resistance, to want to pull back and avoid the hard things that may surface. If you are asking God to help you heal from traumatic experiences, no matter what they are, you need to read the guidelines provided at the end of the workbook. Be gentle with yourself and complete the Self Compassion activity (in the back of the workbook) as often as you need to.

- Be consistent - as I mentioned above, you can expect resistance to arise. When we are serious about walking with God, about walking in freedom, about living in peace and rest we can expect the enemy will try to derail us, but we can also expect resistance from ourselves! Try to set a time and place to work on this, daily if possible. Ask yourself the question, 'What am I doing and why am I doing it?' Write down your answer so you can refer to it when you need to.

- If you fall behind, or don't achieve what you set yourself to do each day, don't quit. Pick it up again as soon as you can. I encourage you to make a specific time to get back into the study rather than telling yourself you'll do it tomorrow or the next day. Refer to the information about setting specific goals that is at the end of the workbook. Most importantly, don't give in to negative, toxic thinking that leads to guilt. That's not from God.

- Be honest with yourself and God as you work through the exercises and answer questions. Knowing the truth about yourself as God's Word tells it will bring freedom to your life that can't be found any other way.

conquering FEAR

> "You can't take fear as a travelling companion if you want to go on a journey with me. I don't travel with fear."
> — Holy Spirit

READ | Chapter 1 of Looking Back Moving Forward

Before I learned to fear I was pushing the limits constantly - even as a toddler. No doubt this contributed to Grandma's grey hair! The fear I'm talking about here is not that adaptive alertness to threats to our safety and wellbeing that God has built into us; the fear I leaned to live with isn't from God. This fear, and the one I discuss in the book, is an intruder, an unnatural invader that has been with man constantly from the moment Adam believed the lies about God and the circle of love and trust was broken. This fear looks for opportunities to barge into our lives and then tramples all over our world. The fear you read about in Conquering Fear was one that led me away from God, away from healing, away from peace and into further self-destruction.

We are going deep here so make sure you read the Guidelines for Writing about Trauma you will find at the end of the workbook in the Resources section. If you find yourself becoming too upset, please stop and talk to someone about what is happening. Get help if you need it.

- **Fear comes in many shapes and sizes. Write a list of everything you associate with fear. This will be different for everyone.**

We know that anxiety disorders are the most common mental health illnesses in the western world, next to depression, and the incidence is increasing.

FEAR AND THE BRAIN

When the fear centre of the brain, the amygdala, is activated, and is not calmed, it triggers a cascade of toxic events which ravage our body and our brain. The sympathetic nervous system activates the release of stress hormones and inflammatory factors. The inflammatory factors wreak havoc in the body causing illness, metabolic problems, and increasing pain. When we live in a constantly stressed state, when fear dominates, our brain becomes severely damaged. In fact, chronic stress turns off the gene that triggers production of a substance called BDNF (I liken it to fertiliser for our brain), so the brain actually begins to shrink in certain areas. These changes have been noted in patients who have a major depressive illness. Fear is a horribly destructive enemy, but it doesn't have to dominate our lives. God shows us the way to deal with fear so it no longer controls us.

GOD'S METHODS

When we use God's methods for increasing brain health and nurturing mental stability - essential for dealing with fear - the damaged brain circuits grow stronger, and despite previous damage, healing happens. Healthy connections grow and develop; our brain changes. If you are someone who suffered abuse during childhood, or if you've struggled with an overactive limbic system resulting in too much aggression, anger, irritability, impatience, selfishness, fear or insecurity, don't be discouraged. God's methods do bring healing.

READ | Romans 12:2 and Ephesians 4:22-24 (Amplified version)

Both the above passages speak of transformation. The transformation comes from the 'constant renewing of the mind.' The verb tense used is present continuous. This means the action is ongoing.

If you struggle with fear in whatever form it shows up in your life:
- What does it mean to you that transformation is ongoing?
- Consider the list you wrote earlier. Now, in the context of that list, consider what transformation means for you? What are you being transformed from? What are you being transformed to? Use the above verses to help you write about what this means specifically to you—don't generalise.

TAKE TIME

Take time each day to reflect on God's Word, on who He is - this will change your brain. Science is showing us through ongoing studies that 15-20 minutes a day of quiet reflection or meditation makes a difference. Often it is too hard to start off with a long period of time, so you can start with just four (4) minutes. Don't make excuses. Just do it! In the Resources section, you will find a script for a four-minute Focus on Breathing exercise. This is a good way to begin to sit quietly for a period of time. The breath is used as an anchor - it's always with you! Your mind will wander because that's what minds do, but every time it does, gently and firmly bring it back to the breath. When you are comfortable with using the breath as something to focus your attention, you can shift to a passage of Scripture, or an attribute of God. Do the same thing as you did with the breath. Every time your mind wanders, just notice that it has, bring it back firmly and continue to focus your attention on what you've decided will be your 'anchor.' We know that what you focus your attention on is what grows.

READ | 1 John 4:16-18 (AMP)

Sometimes our fear comes from how we see God, how we view Him. For me, it was a picture of a vengeful, angry God who wanted to punish me that allowed fear to flourish. Those deceptive brain messages, or toxic thoughts, were based on lies and deception that I had believed from when I was young.

- What is your view of God? Draw, or use words to describe how you see Him.
- The Bible says, many times, that God loves us. Many of us lack this as revelation. Read 1John 1:16 again. This verse emphasises being conscious of His love. Being conscious of something means being actively aware of it - having an ongoing or continuous awareness. It is this active awareness that drives out fear (v18).
- Positive affirmation is a way of renewing your mind and changing your brain. However, the affirmation has to be something that is not contrary to what you know or believe to be true. So, you need to believe what the Bible says, even if you don't yet know it deep within yourself as truth for you. If you believe the Bible to be God's Word and that it speaks truth then choose to say out loud,

"God is love. He loves me and I no longer have to live in fear."

You should make the affirmation daily. Don't wait for fear to strike before you do. The more you say this the more ready you will be to stand on this truth when fear does come against you. Every time you do it, every time you speak it out loud, you are choosing to affirm what is true and what aligns with your True Self - the self that God has created you to be. If you are unsure about how God sees you, go to the Resources section and read the Who I Am in Christ document. As you affirm this, new neural pathways are being strengthened in your brain, and the old toxic pathways become weaker.

READ | 2 Corinthians 10:5

We know our enemy comes to 'steal, kill and destroy' (John 10:10). One way he does this is to sow lies and deception in our mind about God, and about ourselves. These lies and deceptions then become strongholds that guard against us having a true knowledge of God, and of who we are in Christ, of who God has created us to be.

- Read what you wrote earlier about your view of God. Are there any distortions? Any falsehoods? If there are, reread 1 John 4:16-18. Write down, in your own words, what those verses say.

READ | John 8:31-32.

- What/ Who is the Truth?
- How can knowing the Truth help you destroy the strongholds that have set themselves up against the true knowledge of God?

Now consider what your view of yourself is. In my book, I recount that I saw myself as deserving of punishment. I did not like myself and believed I was unlovable, that there was something wrong with me because my parents rejected me. These distortions remained with me and had to be replaced by the truth. This is particularly important if, as a child, there has been abuse. Because of the level of development of the brain when abuse happens in childhood, we misconstrue the meaning of the abuse and internalise distortions about ourselves.

History cannot be changed, but as adults we can re-evaluate the event and apply the truth. The truth is that the awful feelings once experienced belong to the event. Truth brings freedom and healing.

"For God did not give us a spirit of timidity (of cowardice, of craven and cringing and fawning fear), but [He has given us a spirit] of power and of love and of a calm and well-balanced mind and discipline and self-control."

2 Timothy 1:7

EXPRESS YOUR EXPERIENCE

THIS IS WHERE YOU CAN JOURNAL YOUR THOUGHTS FEELINGS AND ANYTHING ELSE THAT YOU HAVEN'T NOTED ELSEWHERE.

understanding LOVE

READ | Chapter 3 of Looking Back Moving Forward

Brain research has discovered that the kind of God you worship changes your brain. It can change it for good, or for bad.

In chapter three of Looking Back Moving Forward I write about how thinking about God as a loving father was hard for me. My experience as a child made it difficult for me to do this. When we distort love and truth we wire perversity into the brain. In a sense, we create 'brain damage.' Brain research has demonstrated that the kind of God we worship changes our brain. The worship of a God of love brings healing. Holding on to lies and deception obstructs the healing process. When we worship distorted characterisations of God - one who is too busy to care, who is detached and disinterested, or who is a cruel tyrant of absolute power who has to be appeased, love is destroyed.

READ | John 15:13

- Jesus' words tell us something about God. **What do they say to you?**

READ | 2 Timothy 3:5

Paul speaks of people who claim to believe in God, but deny the truth about Him, about His character of love. When we have a form of godliness but worship a God who is like Satan alleges (the scary, punitive, distant God), fear increases and over time, we lose our identity, we become shadow people - we live constantly in the shadow of fear; we worship out of fear of punishment, we become afraid to think for ourselves or to question. We end up with a blind faith in an abusive god, which causes us to become like the abusive god we serve. We use our power to control others, to dominate others and coerce others into our way of living. I was doing this through my anger, through closing down, and through refusing to talk.

- **Reflect on the above and write down anything you think is relevant for you.**

Having the right image of God will lead us into blessing, destiny and breakthrough. God wants us to love Him, but before we can do this He first loves us. His love is a gift, and as with any gift, for it to become ours, we need to reach out and take it, to accept it.

READ | James 1:17

God has put us in Christ. We can never earn God's love, but because the Father loves the Son and because both dwell in us, we cannot avoid being loved by God.

READ | John 17:20-26

- Consider the following then write for 5 minutes about what it means to you:

God loves us as he loves Jesus, in exactly the same way.

In Looking Back Moving Forward, I write about how I saw myself. I didn't feel good about myself. I certainly didn't love myself. It's God's nature that allows us to feel good about ourselves. Thanks to His grace we can feel great about who we are, even who we were, and about who we will become. I have learned to love me because God finds me loveable. He finds you incredibly loveable too; He wants you to love yourself as He loves you.

Remember: Jesus paid the price for you to be loved.

The love of God will work on our inadequacies, insecurities and fears - if we allow it to. Love was made to conquer inadequacy and when we live in the light of God's love, inadequacy doesn't matter. When we come alive to the love of God, depending on it for everything in our lives, we trust God to be kind to us, to be for us, not against us (read Romans 8:31) and to 'cause all things to work together [as a plan] for our good' (read Romans 8:28). When we live in this place of love, the Holy Spirit turns our inadequacies into joyful vulnerabilities that bring anticipation rather than dejection. The power of love and compassion can transform our insecurities.

READ | Romans 12:2 and Ephesians 4:23

Our brains are wired for love and connection, so that everything in our brain is geared for healthy, not toxic, thinking. If we allow ourselves to learn fear, it creates chaos and havoc in our brain, and in our lives. But, if this does happen and we allow fear in, as I did, we don't have to stay in that place, in the shadows. We know this because the Bible tells us we can 'be transformed by the constant renewing of our mind'.

All of us long to be loved. God has created us to love and be loved, to be connected to each other, and to care for each other. He created us to be like Him.

READ | 1 John 4:8

- Rewrite the verse in your own words.
- The Bible says that God Is Love. Set a timer and write for 5 minutes about what this means for you.

God first loves us and He demonstrated this by sending Jesus, His Son, to make it possible for us to know His love, to experience it. If someone offers us a gift, we either receive it or we reject it. When we live in fear it can be hard to accept the gift of love. Fear promotes toxic thinking which is made worse by Satan's lies, with the main one being that we don't deserve love, and this gets in the way of us accepting God's wonderful gift.

As long as we think God's love is conditional, we will keep trying to earn it by attempting to prove we are worth loving. When we make mistakes, we feel we are no longer valuable and therefore do not deserve love. We suffer guilt, shame, and the self-condemnation of believing we are not loveable and should be rejected. We keep trying harder and harder until sometimes we are totally exhausted, mentally, emotionally, spiritually and even physically. We try to keep up a good front but inside we are so tired, and very afraid. We can end up with some serious illnesses when we get to this place, and it can be devastating for us. We may even see this as a confirmation that we haven't done enough and God doesn't really care for us.

When we live like this, and don't believe God loves us, we don't love ourselves either. If we don't love ourselves and don't believe ourselves worthy of love we might see this in the following ways:

- You keep falling in love with partners who don't treat you well.
- Or perhaps you have unsupportive friends.
- Or no really close ones.
- No matter what you try, no job fulfils or inspires you.
- And despite countless diets, exercises, makeovers, and cleanses, you still aren't happy with your appearance.
- Maybe certain people in your life drive you nuts. But you can't seem to avoid them.

Whatever the problem is, you keep trying to fix it. But it doesn't go away.

If this is the case for you, if lies are getting in the way of you knowing, believing and accepting that God loves you, and loving yourself, it's time to take a stand. Once we believe God's love is based on who He is and what Jesus has done, and not on what we do, the struggle is over. We know we don't have to 'get' Him to love us, He already loves us, and as we rest in this we can then learn to love ourselves.

God wants us to become familiar with His Word, with what is truth. It is only as we know truth within ourselves that we can then live it out in our life. Recently, researchers documented that positive brain changes are associated with contemplative meditation — but the greatest improvements occurred when participants meditated specifically on a God of love.

> "In this is love: not that we loved God, but that He loved us and sent His Son to be the propitiation (the atoning sacrifice) for our sins."
>
> 1 John 4:10 AMP

WHAT YOU CAN DO

- Read 1 John 4:8-19 out loud. Read it again. Set a timer and write for 5 minutes about what these verses mean to you.

- Read v16 out loud. Being conscious of God's love is being actively aware of it, pondering on it, confessing it out loud. We know that what we focus our attention on is what grows as far as our brain is concerned, so as you focus attention on God's love, as you meditate on it and affirm that God loves you, you will begin to rewire your brain, to create new pathways in your brain that align with truth and your TRUE SELF as God sees you.

- Each morning when you first wake, place a hand over your heart and say, 'God loves me unconditionally.' Try it now. We know that when we do this it stimulates the release of oxytocin, the connection hormone and this causes us to feel loved and valued. God has created us this way, so that as you state those words with your hand over your heart (you may want to close your eyes), this truth will begin to become a part of you, right down to a cellular level.

- Continue to do this daily, and seek out other Scriptures about God's love too. Over time the revelation of God's unconditional love for you will become a reality and that 'conscious knowing' will keep you safe from fear.

- As you learn to believe (as you grow new pathways in your brain) read and write our 2 Corinthians 5:21. Then declare these words daily. Knowing we are loved and accepted even in our imperfection is such a relief! Yes, God is sometimes displeased with our behaviour, but He always loves us. Don't let anything separate you from His love. If thoughts come that try to send you back down that path, label them as deceptive brain messages because they do not align with who God says you are, and don't get caught up in them. It's the knowledge that nothing can separate you from God's love that enables you to be more than a conqueror in life. Read Romans 8:37-38.

We want our confidence and boldness to come from knowing who we are in Jesus, from being secure in God's love for us, His unconditional love. Fear and my distorted view of God drove me to seek this in my work, my education, in the positions I held... and it was never enough.

- **Write a list of everywhere you might be looking for approval, for belonging.**

Once you have your list pray the following prayer:

Father, in Jesus' Name I come to you now and taking your Word as a sharp, two-edged sword I cut myself free from bondage to these things (name each one out loud). I ask you for forgiveness for placing these things before You, and I thank you for that forgiveness and ask that you, Holy Spirit, will guide me in every way as I begin to walk in this new-found freedom into all You have for me. In Jesus' precious Name. Amen.

Everything in this world is shaky. We have seen how things can change in a moment. Even when we are throwing ourselves into work, study, a relationship, our children, the fear is always there '… what if …?' Say the above prayer as often as you need to, to remind yourself that God is your security and your rock. Remember that it takes a while for the new pathways to develop and, while the old pathways become weaker, they are always there so that if you are under stress you might find yourself back in the automatic thinking mode and walking down the old pathway. If that happens, just bring yourself back, pray the prayer and keep moving forward.

READ | Hebrews 13:8

- **What does this verse say?**

We can count on God to be always faithful and do what He says he will do - and He says he will always love us. He says we are righteous in His sight and we need to make a decision to believe it.

- **Take a piece of paper and draw a line down the centre of it.** On one side of the line write 'Who' and on the other, write 'Do.' Under 'Who' begin to list all the aspects of who you are according to God's Word and under 'Do' write all the things you do right and all the things you do wrong. This will help you separate who you are from what you do. Now take a thick pen and cross out the 'Do' list because it has nothing to do with God's love for you. No matter how many right things you listed, you can never do enough to deserve God's love, and no matter how many wrong things you listed they cannot prevent God from loving you.

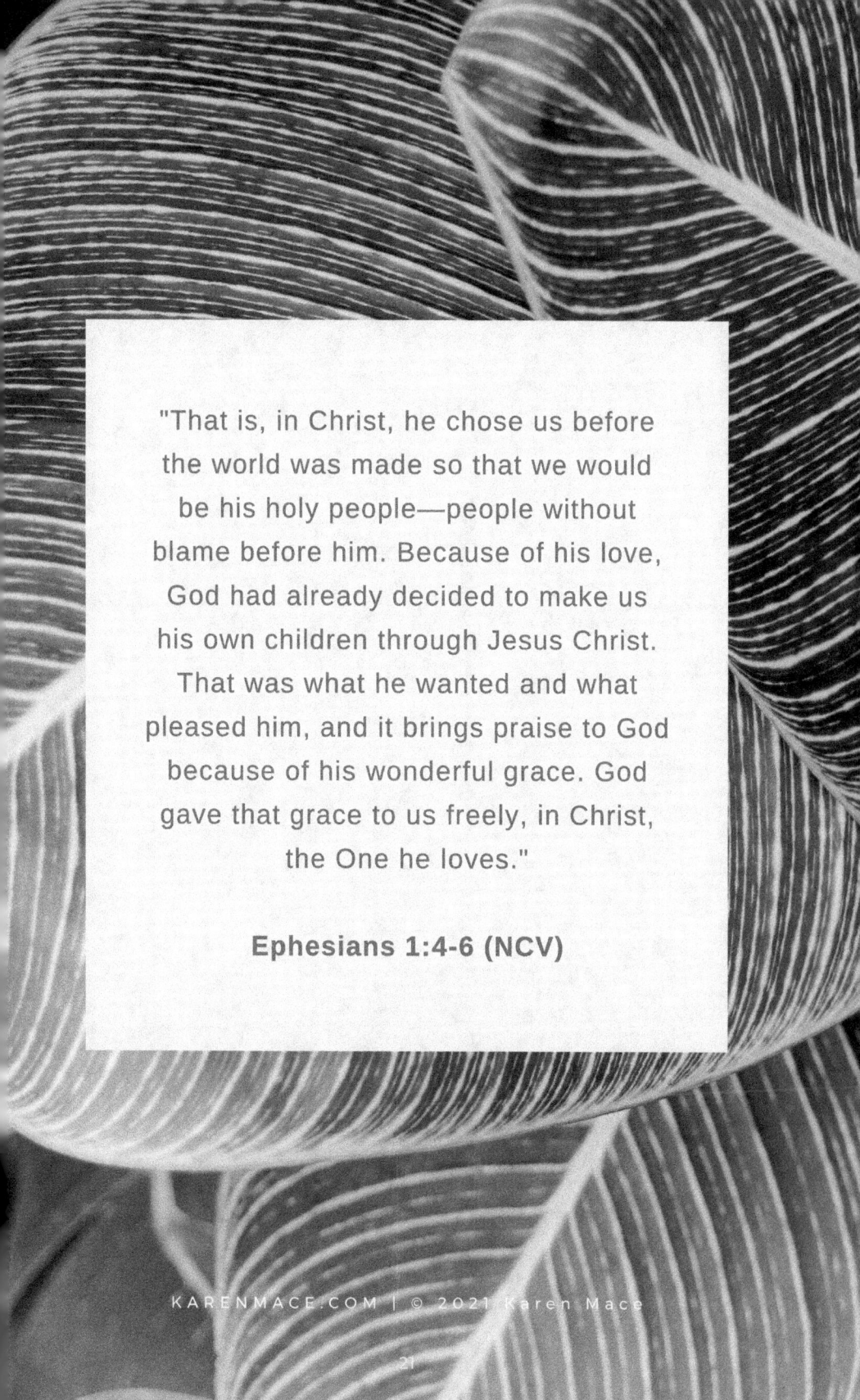

"That is, in Christ, he chose us before the world was made so that we would be his holy people—people without blame before him. Because of his love, God had already decided to make us his own children through Jesus Christ. That was what he wanted and what pleased him, and it brings praise to God because of his wonderful grace. God gave that grace to us freely, in Christ, the One he loves."

Ephesians 1:4-6 (NCV)

EXPRESS YOUR EXPERIENCE

THIS IS WHERE YOU CAN JOURNAL YOUR THOUGHTS FEELINGS AND ANYTHING ELSE THAT YOU HAVEN'T NOTED ELSEWHERE.

finding FREEDOM

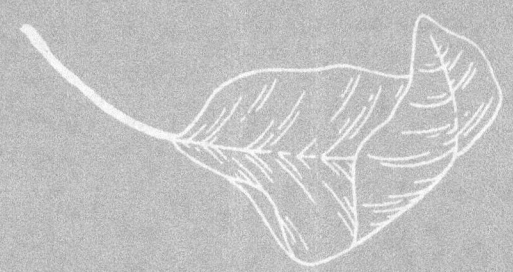

> "Now the Lord is the Spirit, and where the Spirit of the Lord is, there is liberty (emancipation from bondage, freedom)."
>
> **2 Corinthians 3:17 (AMP)**

READ | Chapter 5 of Looking Back Moving Forward

What does it mean to be free? The above verse says it is 'emancipation from bondage...'. For a long time, I lived in bondage although to look at me you would never have known it. I recently watched some of a television series, REIGN. What I noticed most about life in the days depicted was how powerful the king was, but not only that, I also noticed that people who were part of the king's realm were in bondage to the king. It didn't matter if the king was 'mad' - and there have been a few mad kings! It didn't matter if the king was evil or what he was, he controlled the lives of his subjects. They were in bondage to him. It was the kind of bondage that drove William Wallace, the Scottish hero to rise up and seek something better for the Scottish people. He wanted freedom for them; freedom from bondage to the English that had them constantly living in fear for their lives because, on a whim, the person who ruled them could take everything from them, even their life.

What does it mean then, when we talk about bondage as Christians? Here are some verses for you to read. **Write down what each verse says about bondage:**

Romans 8:15	Galatians 4:12
Romans 8:21	Hebrews 2:15
Galatians 2:4	Hebrews 4:2
Galatians 4:8	

Freedom is a word we hear often.

- **Write a list of ten things that freedom means to you. If you are doing this in a group, share your answers. Are they similar? Different? Completely different?**

Freedom means different things to different people, so answers to such a question as the one above will always differ at a personal level. However, on a spiritual level, for those of us who are Christians, whose faith is in God through Jesus, freedom is clearly explained.

- **Read the following verses and write what you believe each is saying about freedom.**

    2 Corinthians 3:17   Galatians 4:31

    Galatians 5:13-15   2 Timothy 1:7

Paul says in Galatians 5:1 that when we are born again in the supernatural, that this freedom in Christ has made us free, it has completely liberated us. And he goes on to say that we are not to 'submit again to a yoke of slavery (bondage).' Once we are free, we are free. But, consider the Israelites when they escaped the clutches of Pharaoh, crossed the Red Sea and finally experienced liberation. They, as yet, had no idea how to be free. In fact, we read in Exodus that their instincts were to return to the place of captivity/ bondage. They were so used to being in bondage that freedom was frightening. Their bondage was more comfortable than the demands of radical freedom. God had to teach the Israelites what freedom meant and the Israelites spent the next 40 years learning to become what they already were: free.

The freedom God gifts us with through Jesus Christ is as radical as the freedom He gifted to the Israelites.

- **Reflect on what 'radical freedom' means to you. To help you to express your thoughts in writing, try the clustering activity you will find in the Resources Section.**

When we come into relationship with God in Christ we come out of bondage into freedom (Galatians 5:1). When the world speaks of freedom, the emphasis is on the individual being free to act as he wishes - usually with the proviso that no one else is hurt in the process. Genuine freedom for the Christian though is different.

READ | Galatians 5:13-14

- The above verse tells us there is 'wonderful' freedom in belonging to God. What does 'wonderful' freedom mean to you?

- What do the above verses tell you about freedom?

- How can serving others be considered freedom?

READ | Ephesians 1:7-10 (The Message version)

- In this paraphrase, the words 'abundantly free' are used. Is there a difference between 'wonderfully' free, 'abundantly' free and 'radically' free? You might like to try the clustering writing activity again. Place the word 'freedom' in the centre bubble. Coming off that bubble, have three separate bubbles, one for each of the words you are reflecting on. If you prefer to draw rather than use words do what is best for you.

When we step into freedom in Christ, we need to unlearn habits and mindsets of the past so we can 'be transformed by the constant renewing of the mind' (Romans 12:2; Ephesians 4:23).

When we are learning something new and different we need help. Learning to live in freedom when we have become used to life in bondage is not easy at first. Like the Israelites, you might find yourself wanting to go back, or even inadvertently slipping back into the old ways. Building new pathways in the brain is like slashing a new path through the jungle. It takes time and effort and then practise to choose the new path, to walk the new walk. And even when the new path is there and seems reasonably well worn, we sometimes, especially when things are challenging and stressful, slip into autopilot and tend to automatically take the old path. But don't despair; God has got your back!

READ | Ephesians 1:4

- What does this verse say about you?

READ | Ephesians 1:13

- What happens when you choose freedom in Christ?

READ | John 15:26

- What are some of the roles of Holy Spirit in your life? How can He help you to learn to live in freedom?

READ | Galatians 5:16

- What does Paul strongly encourage here? Why?

Notice that the verb tense used in Galatians 5:16 is present continuous. Paul doesn't suggest that once is enough. On the contrary, he says we are to 'habitually' walk in the Spirit. This is part of the 'constant renewing of the mind' that leads to our transformation.

We know from scientific studies that our brain can change. It does so when we focus our attention and consistently choose—whether bad or good. The brain doesn't differentiate between good or bad, and God has given us free will to choose. We choose whether to listen to the deceptive brain messages that urge us to go against who we are in Christ, that urge us to choose 'death rather than life' (see Deuteronomy 30:19), or to choose what aligns with our True Self in Christ, as guided by Holy Spirit, our Wise Advocate who is always with us to help us make good choices, to choose life.

READ | Ephesians 4:22-24

Note how v23 is a bridge that takes you from the old way of being (bondage) to the new way of being (transformed). Here again the verb tense used is present continuous - ongoing, not a once only event.

- Now think about your life in the context of freedom and try the writing exercise on the next page.

THE BRIDGE

The following writing exercise is powerful. It can be used over and over, and in various contexts. Try it here in the context of FREEDOM - moving from captivity - however that looks for you, to a place of true freedom that can only be found in Jesus.

STEP 1
You are standing at the edge of a narrow bridge with no rails. Below is a dangerous drop. You want to cross to the other side but the huge drop to rocks and rushing water concerns you. You look back for just a few seconds at what you are leaving behind. Briefly describe this and the feelings that arise as you consider the things you are leaving.

STEP 2
Now, describe the bridge, your surroundings, why you want to cross, how you feel.

STEP 3
You become aware of a person or people on the far bank. They are calling to you. Write about this and the effect on you.

STEP 4
Develop the piece of writing.

You may find yourself returning to this writing exercise at different times throughout your journey. Each time it may be different as you become more confident in the direction you are going. In fact, I suggest that every now and then, you revisit what you write. We tend to focus on how far we have to go rather than how far we have come, so looking back and reading our journal can be very encouraging.

POSITIVE AFFIRMATION

Try the following positive affirmation over the next week. Each morning before you get out of bed:

STEP 1
Breathe out until you feel your lungs empty.

STEP 2
Take a deep breath in and as you do say, 'Praise God, that in Christ I am radically free.'

STEP 3
Breathe out, a long slow breath, and as you do, say, 'Out you go doubt, there is no room for you.'

STEP 4
Repeat this, three times.

> "I will ask the Father, and he will give you another Helper to be with you forever— the Spirit of truth."
>
> John 14:16 NCV

> "Then you will know the truth, and the truth will make you free."
>
> John 8:32 NCV

EXPRESS YOUR EXPERIENCE

THIS IS WHERE YOU CAN JOURNAL YOUR THOUGHTS FEELINGS AND ANYTHING ELSE THAT YOU HAVEN'T NOTED ELSEWHERE.

> "Lean on, trust in, and be confident in the Lord with all your heart and mind and do not rely on your own insight or understanding."
>
> **Proverbs 3:5 (AMP)**

READ | Chapter 9 of Looking Back Moving Forward

'Trust in the Lord with all of your heart...' About the time we were going out to Ecuador, Dion DiMucci had made this verse well known through song. I remember that Ross and I sang it at our farewell. And I remember everyone there singing with gusto. It's easy to say the words and sing the songs when things are going well. And, even when things aren't going well, some people find it easy to trust while others struggle.

READ | Proverbs 3:5-6 (AMP)

- After you read the above verses, set your timer for 5 minutes and write about what the words you read mean to you.

Trust means making yourself dependent on another person for some result or outcome. It's something you can't be forced into and it's a healthy dependency. You have to choose to trust. It's an attitude and it has three parts:

1. You believe in your mind that the other person is trustworthy. List people in your life you consider to be trustworthy. Why do you believe this?
2. The brain changes when we trust. Oxytocin is released when we have an attitude of trust. This is the same hormone that is released when mothers and babies are together. When you are with someone you trust, there is an emotional response. You feel confidence, assurance in trusting this person.
3. You act on what you believe, on your perception of trust. For example, an elderly friend needed someone, a financial planner, to take care of her financial concerns, as she was no longer confident she could manage them. A friend recommended one, and after meeting with him my friend said she believed she could trust him and so she decided to act on this and entrusted him with her finances.

When you trust someone and they offer to help, you don't debate. You believe, you have confidence that the person will do what he or she says, and this is what you respond to.

- **Think of a time when you did this. Write about it here. Describe the situation, the person, and the outcome.**

Trust always involves risk. The other person could let you down. Although all of life involves some risk, when love is involved, you are especially vulnerable. How can you know if you truly trust someone or not? Well, when you truly trust, you don't have a 'Plan B' in case they fail you!

- Consider the above in the context of your relationship with someone close to you. Do you have a "Plan B" just in case?

- Now consider the above in the context of your relationship with God. Do you believe in your heart that God is trustworthy? Why? Why not?

- Do you have assurance and confidence in God? If you do, write about why, and if you don't, write about that.

- If you believe, and you feel confident in God, write about how this trust in Him is evident in your life. How does your behaviour demonstrate that you trust God?

READ | Isaiah 12:2

- **Write what you believe Isaiah is saying about trust here.**

READ | Isaiah 30:15 (AMP)

- **Write about what this means to you.**

Remember, when you choose to do something, your brain recognises this as worth remembering. Every time you choose to trust God, you are 'renewing your mind,' changing your brain for good!

CHOOSING TRUST

- If TRUST were a person, what would he/she be like? Describe TRUST.

Now you know what trust is, you might be thinking you need to renew your mind so you can be transformed in this area of your relationship with God. How will you do this?

- Write down your 'Action Plan' for learning to truly trust God.

- Make a decision now to CHOOSE to trust God.

> "... in quietness and trusting confidence is your strength ..."
>
> Isaiah 30:15 (AMP)

EXPRESS YOUR EXPERIENCE

THIS IS WHERE YOU CAN JOURNAL YOUR THOUGHTS FEELINGS AND ANYTHING ELSE THAT YOU HAVEN'T NOTED ELSEWHERE.

transformation
THE INGING PRINCIPAL

> "...But be transformed (changed) by the [entire] renewal of your mind [by its new ideals and its new attitude], so that you may prove [for yourselves] what is the good and acceptable and perfect will of God, even the thing that is good and acceptable and perfect [in His sight for you]."
>
> **Romans 12:2 (AMP)**

Years ago, when we talked about transformation there would always be someone who said, 'Oh yes, like the caterpillar becoming a butterfly.' The conversation usually shifted after that, we skimmed the surface, not daring, or perhaps not knowing how, to go deep. Transformation is radical, and it has to be when you consider how radical is God's love, His forgiveness, and the freedom He offers us.

Transformation comes through renewing the mind (Romans 12:2; Ephesians 4:23). As we learn to take captive every thought in obedience to Jesus we bring down the strongholds that set themselves up against the true knowledge of God (2 Corinthians 10:5). The strongholds come in the form of 'arguments, theories and reasonings' in our thinking and the behaviours that follow the thinking.

READ | 2 Corinthians 5:17, Colossians 1:21-22 and Titus 3:5

When we come into relationship with God through Jesus, we have work to do. And the work is mainly in the mind. This is where transformation begins. Romans 12:2 says God has a plan in mind for us, His will toward us is good and acceptable and perfect. However, to experience the good things God has planned for us we must actively engage in renewing the mind, which leads to a new attitude.

Before we choose to surrender to God, and Christ becomes our Lord, usually from the time we were tiny, we laid down patterns of beliefs, not only in our brain, but at a cellular level in every part of our being. These beliefs direct our behaviour, our interactions with others and how we see ourselves. When we know Jesus, the strongholds, the core beliefs we have, don't automatically change. I, like many, was totally ignorant of what was needed. I had no idea my thought life needed work. But, if we don't deal with toxic thinking there will be no transformation. We will be stuck.

KARENMACE.COM | © 2021 Karen Mace

CHANGING YOUR THINKING

READ | Chapter 4 of Looking Back Moving Forward

> "Be careful what you think,
> because your thoughts run your life."
>
> Proverbs 4:23 (NCV)

- Can you think of a time when your mind was full of deceptive brain messages? Where the content of your thoughts was doubt, fear, anger, or other negative emotions? Do you have thoughts like that now? Write about this.

God has given us the ability, a wonderful and powerful ability, to quiet our mind, capture our thoughts and focus our attention on what we are doing right now, on the present issue. We live in a world where there are constant demands for our attention so we have moved away from using this natural and necessary ability and instead, we run on autopilot and tell ourselves we are multi-tasking. It is a natural ability because it is wired into the design of the brain allowing the mind to capture and discipline deceptive brain messages (thoughts), and it is necessary because it calms us so that we are in a receptive place where we can hear Holy Spirit guiding us. This ability is often called being mindful rather than being mindless.

Below is a list of some common deceptive brain messages. These are the main types of toxic thinking. Which ones are getting in the way of your transformation? Usually there will be more than one, and often people find a combination at work at the same time. Note the ones that jump out at you as you read through the list.

- All-or-nothing - Believing that something or someone can only be good or bad, right or wrong.
- Catastrophising - Imagining and believing that the worst possible thing will happen.
- Discounting the positive - Devaluing your (or others) positive qualities, attributes, or contributions, or failing to notice the positive reactions someone is having towards you.
- Emotional reasoning - Believing something is wrong with you or your life because you are experiencing uncomfortable emotional or physical sensations generated by different parts of the brain.
- Mind reading - Assuming you know what others are thinking (usually about you).
- "Should" statements - Believing that there are only certain ways to act, behave, or interact with others. (Includes 'ought to' and "must" statements).
- Faulty comparisons - Believing that your current situation is somehow worse than someone else's or how you imagined it would be. When you compare you discount the positive and rely heavily on 'should' statements (among other thinking errors).
- False expectations - Allowing your anticipation of a specific result to negatively affect your brain and body.

READ | Proverbs 23:7

- This verse says that as a man thinks within himself, so he is. Consider this in light of the Deceptive Brain Messages you have marked. Write one paragraph about yourself; be honest about how you see yourself.
- Now on a piece of paper, draw a line making two columns. At the top of one column write 'True Self,' and at the top of the other write 'The Me I See.' In the column under True Self, write down what Scripture says about you. In the other column write how you see yourself. How does your view of yourself align with your True Self, the self that God has created you to be; who you are in Christ?

Often when we are challenged to do something like this our tendency is to avoid it because it brings up feelings of guilt, shame and condemnation. These are deceptive brain messages and are not from God. The best way to deal with them is to face them head on. Remember, that as we move forward in this transformation journey we will meet resistance. That resistance might come from the enemy who does not want you to live in freedom, or it might even come from within you, from those core beliefs you have held within you for so long. It is important to recognise and acknowledge the resistance for what it is, and then to deliberately choose to push through it.

The good news is that our brain can change. We don't have to be stuck in old patterns of toxic thinking that cause so much pain and distress. God tells us to be transformed by the constant renewing of the mind and He has made it possible for us to do that. There is even current research evidence of changes occurring in the brain. Whether the change is for good or bad depends on how we choose. We will focus on the good here. When we focus on an object or belief that is core to our value system we turn on positivity in our brain. What this means is that activity in the emotional centres of the brain is turned down so we experience calmness. However, it is even better when we intensely focus our attention. When we do this, there is a boost in the brain's reward system areas consistent with positive emotions. When these areas are stimulated, dopamine is released, and this is a powerful pleasure neuro-chemical.

What we have learned through the study of spiritual practices is that a clear, conscious intention to immerse yourself in such a practice as worship, or meditation or prayer, can increase feelings of connection and unity with God. This doesn't happen when we do things on autopilot, or out of a sense of duty, or habit. We need to make a choice to deliberately focus our attention on God's Word, His Truth.

It is important to focus on what is an object or belief that is core to your value system. To do that you need to have a good idea of what your values are. Transformation happens in all areas of our life when we work with God and allow Him to change us. To get an idea of where you may want to see change and transformation in your life complete the following activity.

VALUES EXERCISE

In this exercise, you will be asked to look more closely at your personal values in each of four areas and write them out. Then, you will evaluate how close you are to living your life in keeping with your values. You will also take a closer look at the barriers or obstacles in your life that stand between you and the kind of life you want to live. Don't rush through this; just take your time. If you need help you will find a sample in the

IDENTIFY YOUR VALUES

WORK/EDUCATION:

RELATIONSHIPS:

LEISURE:

PERSONAL GROWTH/HEALTH:

SETTING GOALS

When we aren't living according to the values we have, we usually experience guilt, or at the very least extreme discomfort. We Christians have the Holy Spirit to convict us of where we need to change, so this is called 'true guilt' because it moves us towards making a change that is for the better.

- Check in with yourself right now to see whether Holy Spirit is convicting you of an area you need to work on. Write down what that is.

- Write down any barriers that might get in the way of you:
  - living according to your values and / or
  - making any changes Holy Spirit encourages you to make.

Once we are aware of not living according to our values, and of the need to do something about it, it helps to set goals. At the end of this workbook is a resource that can help you as you consider your values and the goals you may want to set.

THE INGING PRINCIPLE

Of course, when we've been so used to living and thinking a certain way, renewing the mind doesn't happen quickly. I've coined a term for the process: the 'Inging Principle'. The 'Inging Principle' is about keeping on, persevering, and it comes from the fact that the verb tense used in Scripture for anything relating to transformation is present continuous - we are transformed and being transformed. We walk in the Spirit and we keep walking in the Spirit (Galatians 5:16). We give thanks and we keep on giving thanks.

Transformation does not begin with what we are not. It begins with the unveiling of who we are in Jesus. God initiates a relationship with us.

READ | Colossians 1:3

- What does this verse say about God?
- What does it say about us?

When God initiates a relationship with us we choose whether we respond or not. It is through the gift of faith that He makes it possible for us to believe.

READ | Ephesians 1:4

- From before time, God knew you, and He chose you in love. Write about how it feels to know that God chose you and has initiated a relationship with you.
- Graham Cooke says that our role is to respond to what God begins in us when He initiates the relationship with us. He says we need to do this through:
    - Acknowledgement
    - Agreement and
    - Abiding
- Write what those three words mean to you in the context of responding to God.
- Once you have done that write how you think you can:
    - Stand in everything God has for you
    - Walk out everything God has for you, and
    - Work out everything God has for you.

Transformation means becoming more like God, more like Jesus. Everything God does in us is with the purpose of making us more like Him. It is ongoing. We are standing, and we continue standing, we are walking out what God has for us and we continue walking it out, we are working out everything He has for us and we continue working it out.

READ | Ephesians 4:21-23

- How is it possible to put on the new nature that is created in God's image? What do we need to do?

READ | 2 Corinthians 3:18

Transformation is ongoing. At salvation God puts us INTO Christ Jesus and from then we are being changed from glory to glory. From that moment, every situation we find ourselves in is about learning how to live in the presence of the Holy Spirit. That's why God gave us the Holy Spirit to be our Teacher, our hope and our Comforter in all life situations.

READ | Deuteronomy 31:8

When we acknowledge all that God is, agree with all God says, and abide in Him, we learn to stand and walk as a lifestyle. We begin like a small child learning to walk and stumble and fall, but each time we get a bit stronger as God draws us to our feet again and sets us on the way we need to go. Transformation carries us forward on our journey with God, and our story unfolds, as we trust Him. He has already been to where you are now. Many years ago, when I struggled in those early days after I turned back to Him, He encouraged me saying, "Take my hand, and put your feet where mine have been. I have already been where I am taking you." When we abide in Him we can let go of fear, anxiety and worry about the present and the future because He has already been to where we are going next.

A major part of walking with God is to know that He never leaves or forsakes us and to know that God can never be disillusioned or disappointed with us. He knows our story and it is He who is taking us on the transformation journey. Nothing surprises Him. When we get that God can never be disillusioned or disappointed with us we come into a whole new place of peace and rest.

Sometimes there are things we need to leave behind as we journey forward into all God has for us.

- The writing exercise The Bridge encourages you to look at what God is calling you to and what He is calling you from. You completed this exercise earlier. Complete it again writing specifically about what God is calling you to leave behind and what He is calling you to.

CRAFTED PRAYER
(FROM GRAHAM COOKE)

We need to realign our thinking so that it is in line with God's thinking. Read the following prayer out loud.

Father,
I know you have already been to today.
I know Jesus is the Author and Finisher of my Faith.
Holy Spirit I know you are my resident genius in teaching and helping me, so I'm pushing away any sense of stress or disillusion with myself or with other people because you have already been here to this part of my story.
So, right now, I'm just going to be still and I'm going to look for You.
I'm going to expect to see your provision for me.
I'm going to love what I'm learning and I'm going to agree with You that there's nothing wrong with me but something must just be missing in my experience of You and You already have every intention of providing it.
So I thank you Holy Spirit that you will help me see it and help me to learn to live in a new level of relationship with You because of this experience.
In Jesus' Name.
AMEN!

ACTIVATION

- Take the above prayer and place it in several places where you will remember to pray it. Don't wait for a difficult day. Realign your thinking expecting God to be in the story of your life, no matter how that looks.

> "The Lord himself will go before you. He will be with you; he will not leave you or forget you. Don't be afraid and don't worry."
>
> Deuteronomy 31:8 NCV

EXPRESS YOUR EXPERIENCE

THIS IS WHERE YOU CAN JOURNAL YOUR THOUGHTS FEELINGS AND ANYTHING ELSE THAT YOU HAVEN'T NOTED ELSEWHERE.

RESOURCES

GOAL VISUALISATION
(TO GET YOU READY FOR WORKING THROUGH THE STUDY)

WHY YOU SHOULD TRY IT

Every day people plan to do difficult things and never follow through - even when it's something we really want to do. You have decided to complete the Looking Back Moving Forward Workbook- yay!! You can do it. But…because we are human, and because we can sometimes sabotage ourselves let's put some things in place to make sure you achieve what you want to achieve.

HOW TO DO IT

1. Make sure the goal/s are something you believe you can reach. Tell yourself 'I can do this' and say it 100 times a day if you need to. Don't allow those toxic thoughts to derail you. You can do this – if you want to.
2. What works is making a vivid, concrete plan. Visualise your goal/s in detail and write it down. What do you see? This is where you make sure what you want to achieve is CLEAR and MEASUREABLE. Also make sure you are REALISTIC. Be specific—you will know what you have to do ahead of time—so, perhaps at the beginning of each week, write down:

- What you need to do, and then make a concrete plan to reach your goal by writing down the following as well:

  - When will you follow through?

  - Where will you do it?

  - How will you do it?

E.g. "Every morning at 8 a.m. I will go into the family room and spend 30 minutes on the study." Or "Tomorrow morning right after I get up, I will sit in the lounge room in the armchair in the corner and do one short section of the study."

GOAL VISUALISATION
(CONTINUED...)

3. Keep a journal of your progress towards your goal and every week look at how far you have come then note this in your journal. This keeps your intention fresh and reminds you of why you are doing what you are doing!

Celebrate each step you take towards achieving the goal/s you have set for yourself. Share your progress with others on the Facebook page. There's lots of evidence that shows encouragement is a great motivator… so if you can connect with others doing the study and just watch how great it is to be encouraged to keep moving forward—encourage someone else regularly too!

If you do this exercise, you are making a growth-mindset plan which makes goals feel attainable and manageable. Concrete plans—plans you can visualise—about how, when, and where you are going to do something lead to really high levels of follow-through, which of course ups the chance of success. When you believe that you will be successful at something, it encourages you to work harder toward achieving that goal—and this greater effort increases the chance that you will actually succeed. Plus, the more you succeed, the more confident you will be about future goals.

4-MINUTE FOCUS ON BREATHING EXERCISE

Begin by finding a comfortable position either sitting in a chair or a cushion on the floor or lying down if you prefer.

Gently closing your eyes.

Taking a moment to check in with how you are feeling right now … allowing yourself to let go of any concerns about the past or future … becoming aware of the feeling of the body sitting or lying here … noticing the areas of contact that the body makes with the chair or the floor … the feet resting flat on the ground, legs supported by the chair, hands resting comfortably on your lap. Taking a deep breath in and gently letting it go … and another deep breath in and letting it go … allowing the breath to flow in and out now in its natural rhythm, not trying to control it, change it in any way … and when you notice your attention has been carried away by thoughts simply letting go of the thoughts and gently directing your attention back to the sensations of the breath. Perhaps noticing as air moves in and out of the nostrils or feeling the belly as it expands on the in breath, falls away on the outbreath. Resting your attention on the breath as it flows in and out. Not thinking about the breath but rather feeling the breath wherever it arises in the body…

Breathing this way has a calming effect on the brain. If you are stressed or anxious it can help. It also helps you to learn to focus your attention and that is useful when we want to meditate on God's Word or simply spend time in His presence.

WHO I AM IN CHRIST

I AM ACCEPTED

John 1:12	I am God's child
John 15:15	I am Christ's friend
Romans 5:1	I have been justified
1 Corinthians 6:17	I am united with the Lord (one Spirit)
1 Corinthians 6:19-20	I am bought with a price; I belong to God
1 Corinthians 12:27	I am a member of Christ's body
Ephesians 1:1	I am a saint
Ephesians 1:5	I have been adopted as God's child
Ephesians 2:18	I have access to God through the Holy Spirit
Colossians 1:14	I have been redeemed and forgiven
Colossians 2:10	I am complete in Christ

I AM SECURE

Romans 8:1-2	I am free forever from condemnation
Romans 8:28	I am assured all works together for good
Romans 8:31-34	I am free from any charge against me
Romans 8:35-39	I cannot be separated from the love of God
2 Corinthians 1:21-22	I am established, anointed, sealed by God
Colossians 3:3	I am hidden with Christ in God
Philippians 1:6	I am confident that God's good work will be perfected in me
Philippians 3:20	I am a citizen of heaven
2 Timothy 1:7	I have not been given a spirit of fear but of power, love, peace
Hebrews 4:16	I can find grace and mercy in time of need
1 John 5:18	I am born of God; the evil one cannot touch me

WHO I AM IN CHRIST
(CONTINUED...)

I AM SIGNIFICANT

Matthew 5:13-14	I am the salt and light of the earth
John 15:1, 5	I am a branch of the true vine, a channel of His life
John 15:16	I have been chosen and appointed to bear fruit
Acts 1:8	I am a personal witness of Christ's
1 Corinthians 3:16	I am God's temple
2 Corinthians 5:17-21	I am a minister of reconciliation for God
2 Corinthians 6:1	I am God's co-worker
Ephesians 2:6	I am seated with Christ in the heavenly realm
Ephesians 2:10	I am God's workmanship
Ephesians 3:12	I may approach God with freedom and confidence
Philippians 4:13	I can do all things through Christ who strengthens me

EXPRESSIVE WRITING

Guidelines for Confronting Trauma in Writing (Louise DeSalvo, 1999)

1. Write twenty (20) minutes a day over a period of four days. Do this periodically. That way you won't feel overwhelmed.
2. Write in a private, safe, comfortable environment.
3. Write about issues you are currently living with, something you're thinking or dreaming about constantly, a trauma you've never disclosed or discussed or resolved.
4. Write about joys and pleasures too.
5. Write about what happened. Write, too, about feelings about what happened. What do you feel? Why do you feel this way? Link events with feelings.
6. Try to write an extremely detailed, organised, coherent, vivid, emotionally compelling narrative. Don't worry about correctness, about grammar or punctuation.
7. Beneficial effects will occur even if no one reads your writing. If you choose to keep your writing and not discard it, you must safeguard it.
8. Expect, initially, that in writing in this way you will have complex and appropriately difficult feelings. Make sure you get support if you need it.

Things not to do when writing:

1. Don't use writing as a substitute for taking action.
2. Don't become overly intellectual.
3. Don't use writing as a way of complaining. Use it, instead, to discover how and why you feel as you do. Simply complaining or venting will probably make you feel worse.
4. Don't use your writing to become overly self-absorbed. Over-analysing everything is counterproductive.
5. Don't use writing as a substitute for therapy or medical care.

CLUSTERING

This is a brainstorming technique. It's a wonderful way to dig deep into your subconscious for ideas and connections you might not normally be aware of.

- Basically, when you cluster, you begin by placing an idea, word, or phrase in the centre of a blank piece of paper then drawing a circle around it. As words and ideas come to mind, you quickly write them down in connected streams or links flowing from the centre circle. You write any and all things that come to mind without censuring yourself, you write until you feel an internal pause, a shift, a feeling that you have written enough for the moment.
- Next, you begin writing about your original topic, about another idea that sprang to mind during the clustering process, or perhaps about something that's not even reflected in the cluster but that seems to be jelled in your mind, ready to burst out.

Short Writing Exercise
Try out the technique of clustering with this short exercise. In the middle of an unlined sheet of paper write the word "JOY." Circle it, think about the word and what joy means to you, and then write down any and all words that occur to you. After you have clustered your initial thoughts, start writing. It can be as long or as short as you'd like.

DEFINING MEANFUL GOALS

CATEGORY	GOAL	How important is this goal? How much meaning does it provide?	How much effort will you put into achieving this goal?
Relationships	Spend more time with my family	10	6 (after competing priorities like work)
Relationships			
Relationships			
Spiritual			
Accomplishments	Stop eating carbs when I am stressed	8	7
Accomplishments			
Leisure/Self-care	Walk every day for 45 minutes	9	6
Leisure/Self-care			

Effort is really important if you are to achieve your goals and competing priorities and desires can derail those efforts. Rate how meaningful each of those goals is to you on a scale of 1 to 10, where 1 = not important at all and 10 = extremely important (a priority in my life). Also rate how much effort you are willing to put forth or which other opportunities you are willing to forgo to achieve each of your goals using a similar scale of 1 to 10, where 1 = will not expend any effort, and 5 = would be willing to work hard/ give up other things 50% of the time, and 10 = will work hard/ prioritise this over everything else 100% of the time. (Use the categories only if they are helpful to you, otherwise list all your goals on another table, but make sure you do not include desires and cravings.)

AFTERWORD

How do you feel now you have finished working through this study? Has it helped you I wonder? As I wrote it, I found it was a great time for me to hear God again. It doesn't matter how many times we do something it seems God is able to bring something new out of it. So, although I have gone over, a number of times, the contents of this workbook, each time God shows me something new that I get excited about. You might find the same if you decide to work through it again.

If you have found Looking Back Moving Forward, and this workbook, helpful, I would appreciate you letting others know about it and also posting something on the Karen Mace Writer Facebook page, as word of mouth really is important in making things known to people.

You can connect with me through my website, karenmace.com or through Facebook, @karenmacewriter, or Instagram, @karenmacewriter.

I know God will bless you as you continue to move forward on your transformation journey.

Karen

Karen Mace

www.ingramcontent.com/pod-product-compliance
Lightning Source LLC
Chambersburg PA
CBHW070729020526
44107CB00077B/2346